The Bible

Inspiration, Interpretation and Right Division

By Roy Ginn

ISBN 978 1 78364 508 4

www.obt.org.uk

****

THE OPEN BIBLE TRUST
Fordland Mount, Upper Basildon,
Reading, RG8 8LU, UK.

The Bible

Inspiration, Interpretation and Right Division

Contents

Preface

Preface

It had been in the back of my mind to produce such a work as this since the earlier part of this century as I had long felt that believers were not being fully taught the value of personal study of the Bible to a degree sufficient enough for them to really get to grips with it and understand its importance and relevance today. I say this from experience.

I had been an active member of a church for about 14 years when I first came across a Bible study magazine that had an unusual approach to Bible study. The writers started with the books of the Bible, gave their understanding of the interpretation of the book being studied, and encouraged the reader to apply it to themselves using the principle of *Right Division*.

This was unusual in that other magazines were looking at the world around them, making social comment, and then throwing in a verse or two at the end to let the reader know that things were going according to God's plan and they therefore need not worry. They started with the world and ended with the Word. This particular magazine started with the Word, and ended with the individual. Although I was aware of the relevant passage concerning right division (2 Timothy 2:15), I was not at all conversant with how it ought to be put into practice.

As a result of continuing to subscribe to this magazine, I began to understand much more about the importance of the Bible, its inspiration and its interpretation, and the necessity of understanding how to rightly divide and apply the Bible to oneself. Personal Bible study is extremely important, but so is the need to undertake it correctly.

It is so important to follow the example of the Bereans (Acts 17:11). The Apostle Paul was directly commissioned by the risen Lord, but that cut no ice with the men of Berea. They did not accept what Paul said, just because he said it. As far as they were concerned the final authority on these matters was the Word of God. That is a principle well worth noting and following for all time.

It is my hope that all who read this will gain a deeper understanding of the value of personal Bible study, of the Bible itself, and of the One with whose breath the Word was given.

Introduction

Introduction

There is a Chapel in the City of London, whose users have a Doctrinal Basis which is expressed in the form of four tenets which are posted on their notice board. They are as follows: -

- The Inspiration of all Scripture.
- The Deity of Christ.
- The absolute necessity for, and all sufficiency of, the One Sacrifice of Christ.
- The necessity to rightly divide all Scripture.

The first three Tenets would most likely be understood and accepted by the majority of the Christian world, but the fourth Tenet does not seem to be as sufficiently grasped as the first three.

For the believer in the Lord Jesus Christ, the study of the Word of God is paramount, for it is the written revelation of God to man. But to understand it correctly, we *must* understand how to 'rightly divide' the word of truth. Failure to do so will only lead to error.

Job was asked the question:

> Can you search out the deep things of God?
> Can you find out the limits of the Almighty? (Job 11:7)

The answer to that, I am sure you will agree, is "No!"

We can only find out God as He chooses to reveal Himself to us. This He has done in His Word, the Bible. So it is vital that we know how to interpret it correctly in order that we may understand it and apply it to ourselves appropriately.

The Interpretation of English Law

The Interpretation of English Law

When looking at the interpretation of English law, there are rules of statutory construction which *must* be applied by the courts. Two of the major rules of interpretation are: -

The Literal Rule.

This dictates that statutes are to be interpreted using the ordinary meaning of the language of the statute. In other words, a statute is to be read word for word and is to be interpreted according to the ordinary meaning of the language, unless it explicitly defines some of its terms otherwise, or unless the result would be cruel or *absurd*. Ordinary words are given their ordinary meaning, technical terms are given their technical meaning, and local & cultural terms are recognized as applicable.

The Golden Rule.

This allows that the grammatical and ordinary sense of the words is to be adhered to, unless that would lead to some *absurdity*, or some repugnance or inconsistency with the rest of the statutory instrument, in which case the grammatical and ordinary sense of the words may be modified, so as to avoid that absurdity and inconsistency, but no farther than that is permissible.

These are the essential rules for the *interpretation* of English law, after which the law can be *applied* appropriately. And these rules *must* be applied strictly. They are not optional!

The Interpretation of the Bible

The Interpretation of the Bible

God's Law, God's Word, on the other hand, appears to be open to all kinds of fanciful interpretation, with no such standards being applied. Surely there is a need to follow some rules of interpretation in order to avoid any misunderstanding? After all, it is only after establishing the correct interpretation that the word can be applied appropriately. So maybe these rules noted above can help us in our quest.

The *Literal Rule* says to give words their literal meaning or sense. The same rule should apply to the interpretation of Scripture. The Holy Spirit says what He means and means what He says. If He says 'Israel', then He means Israel and not 'the church'. To insist on 'spiritualising' a passage will not lead to truth as any number of interpretations may be drawn by any number of readers. The literal sense is the grammatical-historical sense; that is, the meaning which the writer expressed. The vital question is "What does it mean to the people to whom it is spoken or written?"

The *Golden rule* suggests that the literal meaning of words may be departed from if the result of its use produces an *absurd* result.

For Bible study, this means taking the words literally, but also recognising figures of speech, along with the genre of the passage, (which may consist of parable, narrative, poetry, wisdom, gospel, discourse, or prophetic literature). For example, the following is addressed to Israel:

> … I have come down to deliver them out of the hand of the Egyptians, and to bring them up from that land to a good and large land, to a land flowing with milk and honey…(Exodus 3:8)

The Israelites were slaves in Egypt: that is literal truth. The "good and large land" referred to is the land that God promised to Abraham (Genesis 12:1-3; 17:1-8). It was a literal and real land with borders. However, if we were to take the expression "flowing with milk and honey" literally, then that good land would be a very sticky, slushy place to walk through, and I could well imagine many people (and animals) getting many bumps, bruises and broken bones! (Absurd idea). So – we apply the Golden Rule. We recognise the use of a *figure of speech* here, indicating 'a land of fertile pastures'.

God promised Israel a land of abundance and that is what He delivered. The Talmud of Jonathan interprets the Hebrew words *zavat chalav u'dvash*, (flowing with milk and honey) as "milk flows from the goats' [udders], and honey flows from the dates and the figs." Honey here (and elsewhere in the Scriptures) is generally, but not exclusively, understood to be a reference to fruit nectar rather than bees' honey. (A notable exception occurs in Judges 14:8 where bees' honey is clearly meant.)

Fruit trees will grow in many different terrains, but their produce will 'overflow' with nectar *only* when the land is especially fertile, when the trees are particularly well-nourished.

Similarly, livestock can survive in many habitats, but only overflow with milk when they are in particularly fertile pastures. Thus, a "land flowing with milk and honey" indicates a particularly fertile and productive land. (See Genesis 26:12.)

This is what the expression meant to the people of Israel, the people to whom the promise was made. It is important to understand that the way to determine the correct *interpretation* of any passage in Scripture is to determine what it meant to the people to whom it was spoken or to whom it was written. Only after this has been established can the passage be correctly applied. A case of 'interpretation *before* application'.

It should be noted that although there is a single interpretation to be found in each passage, there may be more than one application. However, these applications should stem *from* the interpretation and be guided by what Scripture says elsewhere.

I firmly believe that adhering to the above rules will help you in your quest to read and correctly interpret the Scriptures.

The Inspiration of Scripture

The Inspiration of Scripture

Paul's instruction to Timothy on this matter is:

> But you must continue in the things which you have learned and been assured of, knowing from whom you have learned *them,* and that from childhood you have known the Holy Scriptures, which are able to make you wise for salvation through faith which is in Christ Jesus. All Scripture *is* given by inspiration of God, and *is* profitable for doctrine, for reproof, for correction, for instruction in righteousness, that the man of God may be complete, thoroughly equipped for every good work. (2 Timothy 3:14-17)

The phrase "inspiration of God" is a translation of the Greek word *theopneustos*, which means literally 'God-breathed'. The English Standard Version renders that part of the verse thus:

> All Scripture is breathed out by God. (ESV)

This shows that the Scriptures come from the very mouth of God:

> By the word of the Lord the heavens were made,
> And all the host of them by the breath of His mouth.
> (Psalm 33:6)

This verse equates the word of the Lord with the breath of His mouth.

Peter expresses the same idea:

> ... knowing this first, that no prophecy of Scripture is of any private interpretation, for prophecy never came by the will of man, but holy men of God spoke as they were moved by the Holy Spirit. (2 Peter 1:20-21)

Peter here clearly states that prophecy is not the product of human will, but comes through the Holy Spirit. (It is interesting to note that Peter and Paul, writing in their last letters, both include the subject of the Inspiration of Scripture!)

We need be in no doubt that all Scripture, both Old and New Testaments, is the inspired Word of God.

The principle of Right Division

The principle of
Right Division

The fundamental verse for all interpretation of Scripture is:

> Be diligent to present yourself approved to God, a worker
> who does not need to be ashamed, rightly dividing the
> word of truth. (2 Timothy 2:15)

The Greek word translated "rightly dividing" is *orthotomounta*. It
is made up of two Greek words *orthos* (right) and *temno* (to cut).
The word is used in two places in the Septuagint Version of the
Old Testament. In Proverbs 3:6 it is translated "direct thy paths"
and in Jeremiah 36:23 "he cut it with the penknife". Thus we see
that 'cutting' and 'dividing' are essential ideas of the original
word. When applied, this is what is known as a *dispensational*
study of the Bible. We look to see what applies specifically to us
today, and what we learn from that which is not written to us
today, but has been retained for our learning.

Examples of Right Division

Examples of Right Division

The Lord himself gave us an example of this principle:

> So He came to Nazareth, where He had been brought up.
> And as His custom was, He went into the synagogue on
> the Sabbath day, and stood up to read. And He was
> handed the book of the prophet Isaiah. And when He had
> opened the book, He found the place where it was written:
>> "The Spirit of the LORD *is* upon Me,
>>
>> Because He has anointed Me
>>
>> To preach the gospel to *the* poor;
>>
>> He has sent Me to heal the brokenhearted,
>>
>> To proclaim liberty to *the* captives
>>
>> And recovery of sight to *the* blind,
>>
>> *To* set at liberty those who are oppressed;
>>
>> To proclaim the acceptable year of the LORD."
>
> Then He closed the book, and gave it back to the attendant
> and sat down. And the eyes of all who were in the
> synagogue were fixed on Him. And He began to say to
> them, "Today this Scripture is fulfilled in your hearing."
> (Luke 4:16-21)

If we check back in Isaiah's prophecy, we read:

> The Spirit of the Lord God is upon Me,
>
> Because the Lord has anointed Me

To preach good tidings to the poor;
He has sent Me to heal the brokenhearted,
To proclaim liberty to the captives,
And the opening of the prison to those who are bound;
To proclaim the acceptable year of the Lord,
And the day of vengeance of our God. (Isaiah 61:1-2)

We see from this that the Lord stopped part way through the quotation (verse 2). He stopped after *the acceptable year of the Lord,* and left out the words *and the day of vengeance of our God...* This was a deliberate action on the part of the Lord:

> Do not think that I came to destroy the law, or the prophets. I did not come to destroy but to fulfil. (Matthew 5:17)

Yes, He came to fulfil, but all things are to happen in God's good time, in their due season; and whereas the *acceptable year of the Lord* related to His first advent, the *day of vengeance* relates to His second advent, which is yet to come.

The Lord refers to this at a later time in His earthly ministry:

> But when you see Jerusalem surrounded by armies, then know that its desolation is near. Then let those who are in Judea flee to the mountains, let those who are in the midst of her depart, and let not those who are in the country enter her. For these are the days of vengeance, that all things which are written may be fulfilled. (Luke 21:20-22)

So far, [in 2016], there has been a gap of nearly 2,000 years after the First Advent, and the Second Advent is still a future event.

Now, would Isaiah, reading through his prophecy (Isaiah 61), see any indication of such a time gap between these two events? No! It was hidden in God, only to be revealed in its due season. If God hides a thing, then no man can find it.

Now consider what Peter said on the day of Pentecost, after the Lord's ascension:

> But Peter, standing up with the eleven, raised his voice and said to them, "Men of Judea and all who dwell in Jerusalem, let this be known to you, and heed my words. For these are not drunk, as you suppose, since it is *only* the third hour of the day. But this is what was spoken by the prophet Joel:
> 'And it shall come to pass in the last days, says God,
> That I will pour out of My Spirit on all flesh;
> Your sons and your daughters shall prophesy,
> Your young men shall see visions,
> Your old men shall dream dreams.
> And on My menservants and on My maidservants
> I will pour out My Spirit in those days;
> And they shall prophesy.
> I will show wonders in heaven above
> And signs in the earth beneath:
> Blood and fire and vapour of smoke.
> The sun shall be turned into darkness,
> And the moon into blood,
> Before the coming of the great and awesome day of the LORD.
> And it shall come to pass
> *That* whoever calls on the name of the LORD
> Shall be saved.' (Acts 2:14-21)

If we check back in Joel's prophecy[1], where the quotation comes from, we read:

> And it shall come to pass afterward
> That I will pour out My Spirit on all flesh;
> Your sons and your daughters shall prophesy,
> Your old men shall dream dreams,
> Your young men shall see visions.
> And also on *My* menservants and on *My* maidservants
> I will pour out My Spirit in those days.
> And I will show wonders in the heavens and in the earth:
> Blood and fire and pillars of smoke.
> The sun shall be turned into darkness,
> And the moon into blood,
> Before the coming of the great and awesome day of the LORD.
> And it shall come to pass
> *That* whoever calls on the name of the LORD
> Shall be saved.
> For in Mount Zion and in Jerusalem there shall be deliverance,
> As the LORD has said,
> Among the remnant whom the LORD calls. (Joel 2:28-32)

A study through the book of the Acts will show that the section commencing with the words *I will pour out of my Spirit upon all flesh,* was beginning to be fulfilled, but the later part, beginning

---

[1] For a full discussion of the prophecy of Joel and Peter's use of it on the Day of Pentecost see *Joel's Prophecy: Past and Future* by Michael Penny, published by The Open Bible Trust – see page 80 for details of this publication.

with *and I will shew wonders in the heavens* was not being fulfilled at that time, and was not fulfilled at all during that period. Here we see that the later part awaits the Lord's Second Advent at some future time.

Again, would the prophet reading through his prophecy see any indication of such a time gap between the two events? Again, no! It reads as though both parts will occur together, and Peter quotes the passage as though both parts were beginning to be fulfilled. Now why would he do that if there was no possibility of it happening at that time?

Wrong division – a modern day example

Wrong division – a modern day example

Let us now consider a modern example of what happens when we fail to rightly divide the word of truth - the phenomenon of "Snake Handling".

The following items, taken from the Internet, recall events surrounding Pastors who encourage and practise the handling of poisonous snakes among their congregations:-

16 Feb 2014. A Kentucky preacher famous for handling snakes during religious services has died after being bitten by a poisonous snake at his church.

Jamie Coots was bitten at his church in Middlesboro, Kentucky, and died after he refused to go to the hospital for further treatment.

31 May 2012. Morgantown, W.Va. — A West Virginia Pastor who followed his father into the rare practice of handling snakes *to prove faith in God* died after being bitten during an outdoor service involving the reptiles.

Mark Randall Wolford, 44 – whose own father, also a Pastor, died in 1983 after suffering a fatal bite – had been bitten before and survived. But he died earlier this week after witnesses say a timber rattler bit him on the thigh. Wolford's sister, a freelance photographer told media outlets it happened during a Sunday service at Panther State Forest.

The basis for the practice is based on Jesus' promise to the Eleven, recorded in Mark's gospel:

> And these signs will follow those who believe: In My name they will cast out demons; they will speak with new tongues; they will take up serpents; and if they drink anything deadly, it will by no means hurt them; they will lay hands on the sick, and they will recover. (Mark 16:17-18)

How extraordinary that people pick out the part of these verses that refers to taking up serpents, but then ignore the parts before and the parts that follow! If they pass around the poisonous snake, should they not also pass around the poisonous drink as well? If they were also laying hands on the sick that they may *recover*, then how come the pastors died?

They failed to rightly divide the word of truth. A read through the Acts of the Apostles shows that these things did happen during that period (though no example is seen of drinking anything deadly). But after Israel was set aside by God at the end of the Acts period, evidential miracles also ceased. Even the Apostle Paul was unable to cure Timothy of his infirmities, advising him instead to take wine for his stomach's sake and his frequent infirmities (1 Timothy 5:23). He also had to leave Trophimus in Miletus sick (2 Timothy 4:20).

Reading the Bible

Reading the Bible

Miles Coverdale [at the front of his translation] offered some invaluable advice about how to read the Scriptures, when he said:

> It shall greatly help ye to understand the Scriptures if thou mark not only what is spoken or written, but of whom and to whom, with what words, at what time, where, to what intent, with what circumstances, considering what goeth before and what followeth after.[2]

This gives us a clue as to how to rightly divide the Word of God. It is important to see to whom a portion of the Word of God is addressed.

To whom is it spoken or written?

Isaiah tells us that his book concerns Judah and Jerusalem (Isaiah 1:1).

This prophecy was not written to us, or about us, so we should not appropriate promises God has made to Judah, or warnings He has given to them, to ourselves, and then 'spiritualise' them to make them applicable for us today. This is *not* rightly dividing the Word.

---

[2] For a full treatment of these words by Miles Coverdale see *Approaching the Bible* by Michael Penny, published by The Open Bible Trust – for details of this publication see page 76.

James commences his epistle by telling us that he is writing to the twelve tribes which are scattered abroad (James 1:1). This epistle is not written to the Church of the One Body, but is written directly to the people of Israel.

In his first epistle, Peter tells us that he is writing to the Pilgrims of the Dispersion (1 Peter 1:1). These are Israelites who live outside of Israel.

Those addressed were Peter's own people. The church of which Christ is the Head is not *a chosen generation, a royal priesthood, a holy nation, a peculiar people* (1 Peter 2:9), for this is a quotation from Exodus 19:5-6. The Law, *the oracles of God*, was given to Israel, and not to any Gentile nation (Romans 3:1-2).

It is important to see to whom the book is written in order to be able to interpret it correctly. So if that is the case, do we need to read these books today? Paul makes a pertinent point:

> For whatever things were written before were written for our learning, that we through the patience and comfort of the Scriptures might have hope. (Romans 15:4)

Note the use of the word FOR. The Old Testament Scriptures were not written TO us or ABOUT us, but were written FOR our learning. The same goes for a large part of the New Testament too, for that was also addressed to, or relates to, Israel.

I remember reading an article in a magazine a few years ago. It was a letter written by a father to his son. The father had started a business with one kiosk, undertaking shoe repairs. Over the years the business had grown into a large organisation, undertaking shoe repairs and key-cutting, with a multi-million pound turnover, and the father was then ready to retire. The letter was about his thoughts as he prepared to hand over the business to his son.

Why was the letter reproduced in this magazine? Quite simply, it was for our learning – for all who read the magazine. It was not addressed to us, nor was it about us. So, what could we learn from this letter?

Well, we could learn about the father. We could learn about the son. We could learn about the father's business. These were the main elements of the letter. But where it has personal comments, such as a reference to "handing over the keys of the business to you" on such-and-such a day at such-and-such a time in such-and-such a place, do I think, "Oh, he's handing over the keys to me"? Of course not, because it was not written TO me or ABOUT me. You see the point?

So, if a part of the Bible is not written to me or about me, but is written *for* my learning, what should I be looking to learn? I think first and foremost we must be looking to learn about God and to learn about Christ. The Lord, in prayer, said:

> And this is eternal life, that they may know You, the only true God, and Jesus Christ, whom You have sent. (John 17:3)

Here the Lord equates eternal life with knowing God and knowing Christ. How important then is this topic? Thus, the first thing we look for when reading the Word of God is: -

"What does it teach me about God?" and "What does it teach me about Christ?" This is the first and most important thing to learn. If you get this wrong then you fall at the first hurdle.

John's gospel records the Lord saying to the Jews:

> You search the Scriptures, for in them you think you have eternal life; and these are they which testify of Me. (John 5:39)

Again, in Luke's gospel we read the account of two people on the road from Jerusalem to Emmaus. The risen Lord drew near to them as they walked and asked about their conversation. Then we read:

> And beginning at Moses and all the Prophets, He expounded to them in all the Scriptures the things concerning Himself. (Luke 24:27)

How blessed those two were! They were chosen from among all the disciples to experience having the Lord open the Scriptures to them. They heard the written Word expounded by the Living Word. What was His choice of topic? Himself! Blessed indeed were they.

Again, we read of Paul addressing Timothy:

> … and that from childhood you have known the Holy Scriptures, which are able to make you wise for salvation through faith which is in Christ Jesus. (2 Timothy 3:15)

At the time when these three statements were written about the Scriptures, there was no New Testament in existence. It was the Law, the Prophets and the Psalms that were being referred to in each case.

So we can expect to learn of Christ in the Old Testament. We can also expect to read the great truths of Salvation through Christ in the Old Testament – redemption, atonement, substitution, sanctification, and much, much more.

Paul reminds his readers in Corinth of the time when Moses lead the children of Israel out of Egypt, and of some of the things which followed:

> Now all these things happened to them as examples, and they were written for our admonition, upon whom the ends of the ages have come. (1 Corinthians 10:11)

Paul sheds further light on this subject in his letter to the Hebrews:

> For the law, having a shadow of the good things to come, and not the very image of the things, can never with these same sacrifices, which they offer continually year by year, make those who approach perfect. (Hebrews 10:1)

Thus, we can expect to find *Types and Shadows* in the Old Testament. What are they?

The word "type" in the Greek, is the word *tupos*. This word is used for a die (as something struck). It is derived from the verb *tupto,* to thump or to hammer with repeated blows of the fist or palm. By implication it came to mean a stamp or scar, and from this by analysis it was used for a shape, a statue, a style or resemblance. It has the sense of a model or standard; the mark or impression of something; *or a figure or representation of something to come.*

In the Bible, a type may be a person, a thing, or event, so fashioned as to resemble another, i.e., the *Antitype*. The antitype is the thing it resembles. A type may be:

A person:

> Nevertheless death reigned from Adam to Moses, even over those who had not sinned according to the likeness of the transgression of Adam, who is a type of Him who was to come. (Romans 5:14)

So *Adam* is a type of Christ. He is a type by *contrast*:

> For as by one man's disobedience many were made sinners, so also by one Man's obedience many will be made righteous. (Romans 5:19)

Adam's disobedience brought sin and death – Christ's obedience brought righteousness and life.

Isaac is a type by *comparison*. There are many examples, but the following are just a few.

Isaac	Christ
A child of promise (Gen. 15:4; Gal. 4:28)	A Child of promise (Isa. 7:14)
Birth pre-announced to Sarah by an angel (Gen. 18:10)	Birth pre-announced to Mary by an angel (Luke 1:30-31)
Emphatically called "an only son" (Gen. 22:2; Heb. 11:17)	Emphatically called "An only Son" (John 3:16)
Carried the wood on which he was to die (Gen. 22:6)	Carried the cross on which He was to die (John 19:17)
Went willingly to the altar (Gen. 22:9)	Went willingly to the cross (Jn.10:17)
Rose from the place of death in resurrection (Heb. 11:17-19)	Rose in glorious resurrection from the dead (Matt. 28:6)

- A type may also be a *thing*, such as the Tabernacle, the Temple, the Cities of Refuge, the Pillar of fire/cloud, the Manna.
- A type may be an *event*, such as the Passover, the Day of Atonement or the crossing of the Red Sea.
- The Levitical Offerings are types, and the garments of the high priest can be viewed in the same way.

Time does not permit a detailed study here, but I believe you will find rich blessings in examining the lessons offered for our learning.

Finally, in this section, we should look again at Paul's assertion to Timothy:

All Scripture is given by inspiration of God, and is profitable for doctrine, for reproof, for correction, for instruction in righteousness. (2 Timothy 3:16)

All scripture is profitable for what we need. Think of the definitions that follow:

- Doctrine – Putting people on the right track.
- Reproof – Pulling people up when they go off the right track.
- Correction – Putting people back on the right track.
- Instruction in righteousness – ensuring people continue on the right track.

No wonder the Psalmist could say: -

Your word *is* a lamp to my feet,
And a light unto my path. (Psalm 119:105)

How can a young man cleanse his way?
By taking heed according to Your word. (Psalm 119:9)

Open my eyes, that I may see
Wondrous things from your law. (Psalm 119:18)

What a treasure we have in this book! There is much to learn in all Scripture. If we have the same attitude as the Bereans (Acts 17:11) we will accept that all Scripture is inspired of God and is profitable, but can only be profitable if rightly divided.

Paul tells his readers in Hebrews:

> For the word of God *is* living and powerful, and sharper than any two-edged sword, piercing even to the division of soul and spirit, and of joints and marrow, and is a discerner of the thoughts and intents of the heart. (Hebrews 4:12)

And to the Ephesians, describing the armour of God, Paul says:

> And take the helmet of salvation, and the sword of the Spirit, which is the word of God. (Ephesians 6:17)

The sword of the Spirit – the word of God! That was the weapon used by the Lord when faced by the Tempter after 40 days in the wilderness (Luke 4).

How important it is to know how to handle this sword correctly!

What is spoken or written?

Miles Coverdale noted that it was important to mark what is spoken or written. I touched on this briefly when referring to the interpretation of English law. What words are being used? And what do they mean, literally?

I want to look at some very important examples of this. The word 'Church' is much misunderstood, and careful attention should be paid to its usage.

The Church

It is common for believers today to think that there is only one church, i.e. the 'body of Christ' (Colossians 1:24) which, they say, began at Acts 2, and continues today. However, this is a misconception. The Greek word translated 'church' and 'assembly' is the word *ekklesia*. It is made up of two words: *ek* 'out of' and *kalein*, 'called or summoned'. The word itself simply means 'a called out company'. It will therefore be important to note the context in which the word is used in order to determine what kind of an assembly it is that is being called out.

The following are examples from the N.T: -

> This Moses whom they refused, saying, "Who made thee a ruler and a judge?" the same did God send *to be* a ruler and a deliverer by the hand of the angel which appeared to him in the bush. He brought them out, after that he had shewed wonders and signs in the land of Egypt, and in the Red sea, and in the wilderness forty years. This is that Moses, which said unto the children of Israel, "A prophet shall the Lord your God raise up unto you of your brethren, like unto me; him shall ye hear." This is he that was in the church in the wilderness with the angel which spake to him in the mount Sina, and *with* our fathers: who received the lively oracles to give unto us. (Acts 7:35-38, KJV)

The verses above show that the Church in the Wilderness relates to the people of Israel called out of Egypt.

The Lord refers to a different church when addressing Peter:

> And I also say to you that you are Peter, and on this rock I will build my church; and the gates of hades shall not prevail against it. (Matthew 16:18)

This church is related to the 'Kingdom of Heaven', and is entrusted to Peter. He was given the keys to this church. He was the one who would 'open the doors' to the Gentiles, that they may enter in. (See the early chapters of the book of Acts). This kingdom is a future kingdom which is heavenly in character, but will be located on the earth. It is the kingdom of the Lord's Prayer.

> Your kingdom come.
> Your will be done
> On earth as it is in heaven. (Matthew 6:10)

Paul, addressing the elders at Ephesus, said: -

> Therefore take heed to yourselves and to all the flock, among which the Holy Spirit has made you overseers, to shepherd the church of God which He purchased with His own blood. (Acts 20:28)

This is the 'church' which Paul "persecuted" (1 Corinthians 15:9). This was the 'church' which began on the Day of Pentecost, as seen in Acts 2.

These churches of the Acts period were foundationally Jewish, with Gentiles added to them, or grafted in (Romans 11:17). The churches spoken of after the Jews were set aside at the end of the Acts period are again different, being independent of Israel.

After the end of the Acts Period, Paul wrote in his letter to the Ephesians:

And He put all things under His feet, and gave Him to be head over all things to the church, which is His body, the fullness of Him who fills all in all. (Ephesians 1:22-23)

Colossians refers to the same church: -

And He is the head of the body, the church, who is the beginning, the firstborn from the dead, that in all things He may have the pre-eminence. (Colossians 1:18)

I now rejoice in my sufferings for you, and fill up in my flesh what is lacking in the afflictions of Christ, for the sake of His body, which is the church. (Colossians 1:24)

This is the church which is called 'The Body of Christ' (Colossians 1:18,24), and of this church, Christ is the Head. This church came by special revelation to the Apostle Paul. We do not know when the Apostle received this revelation, but it appears that while he was a prisoner at Rome (Ephesians 3:1), he was given authority to make it known.

The Church of the 'one body' is foundationally Gentile with Jews added on an equal basis.

But now in Christ Jesus you who once were far off have been brought near by the blood of Christ. For He Himself is our peace, who has made both one, and has broken down the middle wall of separation, having abolished in His flesh the enmity, that is, the law of commandments contained in ordinances, so as to create in Himself one new man from the two, thus making peace, and that He might reconcile them both to God in one body through the cross, thereby putting to death the enmity. And He came and preached peace to you who were afar off and to those who were near. For through Him we both have access by one Spirit to the Father. (Ephesians 2:13-18)

This church did not begin at Acts 2, but began after Israel was set aside by God at Acts 28 (see v 23-29). It is spoken of as one new man (Ephesians 2:15); something never seen before, which is not said of any other church.

From this we can see how important it is to always ask what church is being referred to in the passage we are reading. Otherwise things that pertain to one church may be read into another to which it does not belong.

Likewise, there is more than one gospel in Scripture, and differences should be noted carefully. In Galatians 2:7 we read of the "gospel of the circumcision" and the "gospel of the uncircumcision". If these two are the same, why the need to distinguish them?

When was it spoken or written?

A distinct time element is revealed in Scripture by the use of the Greek word *katabole,* translated by the English word 'foundation'.

Seven times we have the time element *apo katabole* – 'from (or since) the foundation' (Matthew 13:35; 25:34; Luke 11:50; Hebrews 4:3; 9:26; Revelation 13:8 and 17:8).

Three times we have the time element *pro katabole* – 'before the foundation' (John 17:24; Ephesians 1:4; 1 Peter 1:20).

From these passages we see that there were certain things that took place "***from*** the foundation of the world" such as, Kingdom parables, Kingdom prepared, Blood of prophets, Creation works, Suffering endured, Lamb slain, Names in the Book of Life.

There were also certain things that were ordained "***before*** the foundation" – Christ loved before, Members of the Body of Christ chosen before, and Christ foreordained before to be a Lamb.

Writing to the Corinthians, Paul says:

> However, we speak wisdom among those who are mature, yet not the wisdom of this age, nor of the rulers of this age, who are coming to nothing. But we speak the wisdom of God in a mystery, the hidden wisdom which God ordained before the ages for our glory, which none of the rulers of this age knew; for had they known, they would not have crucified the Lord of glory. (1 Corinthians 2:6-8)

This predetermined secret had to do with Christ and the cross as the context reveals. Paul is contrasting this wisdom of God with the wisdom of men who reject the essential place of the cross (See 1:20; 2:6, 8; 3:19).

Mathew 24:15,16,21; Colossians 3:4; 1 John 3:2 make it plain that there is a time for the fulfilment of every promise or prophecy. So what may be truth at one time may be error at another.

To everything there is a season,
A time for every purpose under heaven. (Ecclesiastes 3:1)

The time that a thing was spoken, or the time that is referred to, will have a bearing on its interpretation.

The same is true of the place referred to.

Where?

The Scriptures set forth *three distinct future spheres of blessing*, namely: The Earth, The New Jerusalem and The Heavenly Places. The New Jerusalem comes down from heaven and has its final resting place on the New Earth. (See Revelation 3:12 and 21:2,10.)

It is important to note that these are three distinct spheres of blessing and should not be confused one with another.

Certainly it is true that every calling of God rests upon the one sure foundation, (1 Corinthians 3:11; Acts 4:12).

The Earth

> Now I saw a new heaven and a new earth, for the first heaven and the first earth had passed away. Also there was no more sea. (Revelation 21:1)

At some future time there will be a new heaven and a new earth wherein dwells righteousness. Both John and Isaiah tell us that the former things will not be remembered, nor come into mind (Revelation 21:4; Isaiah 65:17).

The New Jerusalem (The Heavenly Calling)

> But now they desire a better, that is, a heavenly *country*. Therefore God is not ashamed to be called their God; for He has prepared a city for them. (Hebrews 11:16)

This refers to that "better country" in which is situated the city for which Abraham looked (Hebrews 11:10), which is the hope of the "heavenly calling" (Hebrews 3:1).

This calling consists of Jews and Gentiles blessed with faithful Abraham (Galatians 3:9 and 14). These are the "heirs according to the promise" (Galatians 3:16, 18 and 29). They are also referred to as "the Israel of God" (Galatians 6:16), and citizens of the Heavenly Jerusalem (Hebrews 12:22; 13:14) which is above (Galatians 4:26), and the Bride, the Lamb's wife (Revelation 21:2,9,10).

The Heavenly Places

> Blessed *be* the God and Father of our Lord Jesus Christ, who has blessed us with every spiritual blessing in the heavenly *places* in Christ. (Ephesians 1:3)

The church which is His Body, and of which He is the Head, is seated with Christ. This is the place where Christ is seated today (Ephesians 1:20; Colossians 3:1) and where those of this calling are seated (Ephesians 2:6). Christ is Head now to the One Body in the heavenly places. When He is manifested in glory those of this calling will be manifested with Him (Colossians 3:4).

So there are three callings and three spheres of blessing associated with them. To understand the Scriptures we must rightly divide according to times and places and spheres of blessing.

Other helpful principles

Other helpful principles

Every text has its context, and no individual scripture (or part of Scripture, as in the snake handling preachers), should be interpreted apart from its context, otherwise we cannot hope to find truth.

Principle of First Occurrence

This rule suggests that the very first time any important word is mentioned in the Bible that occurrence gives the clue to that word's most complete, and accurate, meaning. It not only serves as a 'key' in understanding the word's Biblical concept, but also to providing a foundation for its fuller development in later parts of the Bible.

For instance, in Genesis 6, we have the first mentions of Grace (v8), Righteous, [Just] (v9), Atonement [Pitch] (v14), and Covenant (v18). When you choose to study these great words of faith, it will help you to do so by studying the context of the first occurrence of the word. For example, let us look at the first occurrence of *Sanctification:*

> Then God blessed the seventh day and sanctified it, because in it He rested from all His work which God had created and made. (Genesis 2:3)

The Hebrew word translated 'sanctified' comes from word *qodesh*[3]. Together with the Greek word *hagios* it is variously translated by such words as, sanctify, consecrate, dedicate, holy, holiness and sanctification. The basic meaning of sanctification is 'to set apart'. This separation is always for the service and glory of God. In the first occurrence of the word we can see that God set apart the seventh day as a day of rest, because in it He rested. This gives you the key to all usage of the word.

> Now take Aaron your brother, and his sons with him, from among the children of Israel that he may minister to Me as priest, Aaron and Aaron's sons: Nadab, Abihu, Eleazar, and Ithamar. And you shall make holy garments for Aaron your brother, for glory and for beauty. So you shall speak to all who are gifted artisans, whom I have filled with the spirit of wisdom, that they may make Aaron's garments, to consecrate him, that he may minister to Me as priest. (Exodus 28:1-3)

The word is here translated 'consecrate'.

From the first occurrence we know that consecrate means 'to set apart', and in these verses we see Aaron and his sons being set apart to serve as priests before God. And so the theme remains constant throughout the Word of God.

Principle of testing the things that differ

This is an important principle by which we should divide the word of Truth so as to make a distinction where God places one:

---

[3] The actual word is *wayyeqadesh* which means 'he sanctified'.

And this I pray, that your love may abound still more and more in knowledge and all discernment, that you may approve the things that are excellent ... (Philippians 1:9-10)

The Companion Bible note on this states that "are excellent = differ". It then goes on to say "We are to test the things and having found them to differ, must not join them together, but rightly divide them (2 Timothy 2:15)". Now this is sound advice.

Paul had been praying for the Philippians, that their love may abound more and more in knowledge and in all judgement, in order that they may try the things that differ and so approve the things that are excellent. This can be seen in the following examples: -

- Paul healed everyone on Malta (Acts 28:9), but later left Trophimus sick at Miletus (2 Timothy 4:20).
- Paul sent handkerchiefs to heal people in Acts, but later sent Timothy only advice. (1 Timothy 5:23).
- In 1 Corinthians 7:26-28 Paul advised people not to get married and not to have children (due to the present crisis) but afterwards he advised them to get married and have children (1 Timothy 5:14).

Now there are things in Scripture which seem like each other, but are actually different. You may have been told that things which are different are actually the same (i.e. 'Israel' and 'The Church'). However, if you do not examine the things that differ to see if that is the case, then confusion and error will result.

We have looked at the occurrences of the word 'church' earlier, and seen that the "Church *in the Wilderness*", is different from the "Church *which is His body*", and it would clearly be erroneous to say that these two represent the same company of people. The two are clearly separate.

As another example, look at 'law' and 'grace':

> For the law was given through Moses, *but* grace and truth came through Jesus Christ. (John 1:17)

Here we see a contrast between 'law' and 'grace'. By 'law' we mean that legal system instituted by God to Moses through angels at Mount Sinai (Exodus 20). By 'grace' we mean that unmerited favour of God bestowed upon all men in Jesus Christ at Calvary.

Scripture never mixes 'law' and 'grace'. They are always kept distinct. 'Law' is a ministry of condemnation; 'grace' a ministry of consolation. 'Law' curses; 'grace' redeems from the curse. 'Law' kills; 'grace' makes alive. This is made clear in the Epistle to the Romans:

> But now the righteousness of God apart from the law is revealed, being witnessed by the Law and the Prophets, even the righteousness of God, through faith in Jesus Christ, to all and on all who believe. For there is no difference; for all have sinned and fall short of the glory of God. (Romans 3:21-23)

'Law' in its principle demands righteousness from man; while 'grace' in its principle gives righteousness to men. They have principles that differ. They also have purposes that differ. The

Law of Moses was never given to save men, but that men might know the exceeding sinfulness of sin and the exceeding helplessness of all human effort, and hence lead them to Christ as the only way of salvation. (Romans 7:7, 13; Galatians 3:24). Before the Law was given there was sin in the world, but when the Law was introduced it made sin a transgression and the sinner a transgressor (Romans 4:15; 5:20; Galatians 3:19).

To sin is to 'fall short' of the mark (Romans 3:23). To transgress is to 'step over' the mark.

If you see a sign saying "Please keep off the grass" then if you step on the grass, you commit a trespass and it becomes a transgression and you a transgressor. But before the sign, it was indeed wrong to trespass; but it was not a transgression.

There are other things that differ that may appear to be the same, such as faith and works. These all must be tested to see if they differ, and where this is so, the distinction must be maintained.

Conclusion

Conclusion

My aim here has been to demonstrate, in some small measure, how essential the Word of God is to all men everywhere. I trust you have seen that the Word of God is divinely inspired and that it needs to be 'rightly divided' in order to be correctly interpreted. I trust you have also picked up some useful tips on how to delve into the depths of its riches and so to learn more of God and of the Lord Jesus Christ, who said:

> "It is written, 'Man shall not live by bread alone, but by every word that proceeds from the mouth of God.'" (Matthew 4:4)

About the author

Roy Ginn was born in London in 1955 and spent most of his early life in Bromley where, as a teenager, he began to attend a church youth club and in 1969 became a believer in Christ. Two years later he left school and began a career in banking and moved to Birmingham in 1980. It was during his years there that he became acquainted with right division.

In 1988 he moved to Newcastle-upon-Tyne and after several jobs there entered the university, graduating in Accounting and Mathematics, before returning to the London area and continuing to work in the accountancy field. He retired in 2016 and lives in Essex with his wife Lynette.

Also by Roy Ginn

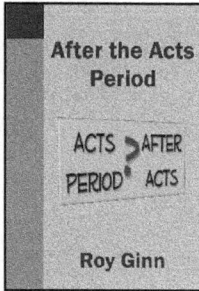

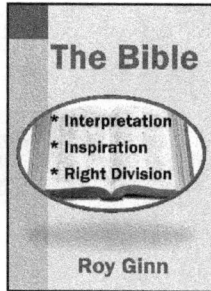

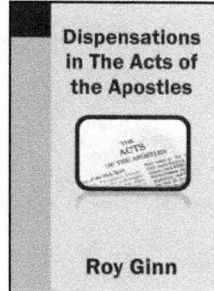

After the Acts Period

ACTS > AFTER
PERIOD° ACTS

Roy Ginn

The Bible

* Interpretation
* Inspiration
* Right Division

Roy Ginn

Dispensations in The Acts of the Apostles

Roy Ginn

The Bible: Interpretation, Inspiration, Right Division.
After the Acts Period
Dispensations in The Acts of the Apostles

Further details of these can be seen on

www.obt.org.uk

These are available as paperbacks from that website and also from

The Open Bible Trust
Fordland Mount, Upper Basildon,
Reading, RG8 8LU, UK.

They are also avaialble as eBooks from
Amazon Kindle and Apple.

They are also available as KDP paperbacks from Amazon .

Also on this subject

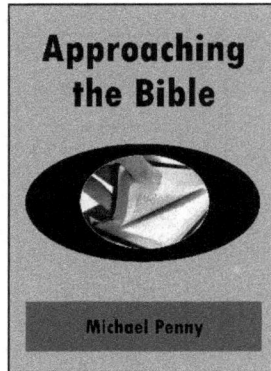

Approaching the Bible
Michael Penny

This book clearly explains how we need to approach the Bible if we are to make sense of what God has said. It does so in an easy to read style and with an easy to understand method. Michael Penny does an excellent job of following the advice of Bishop Miles Coverdale, which was contained in the first Bible printed in English.

That advice was based on asking such questions as:

- "Who" were these words written to, or "Who" were they about?
- "Where" is this to take place?
- "When" was it written or "When" is it about?
- "What", precisely, is said?
- "Why" did God say it, do it, or will do it?

After asking such questions, then we will have a better understanding of the Bible and can "Apply" that passage to our lives today.

****

Further details of this book can be seen on

www.obt.org.uk

It is available as a paperback from that website and also from

The Open Bible Trust
Fordland Mount, Upper Basildon,
Reading, RG8 8LU, UK.

It is also avaialble as an eBook from
Amazon Kindle and Apple.

It is also available as a KDP paperback from Amazon

.

THE FOUNDATIONS OF DISPENSATIONAL TRUTH

E W Bullinger

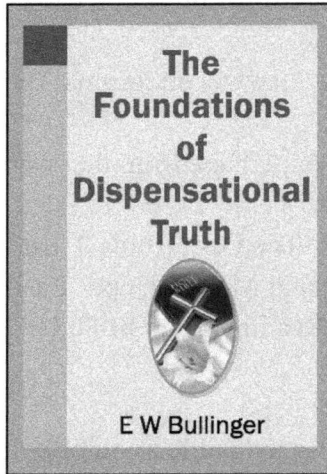

This is Bullinger's last book and is his definitive work on the subject of dispensationalism. It covers the ministries of ...

- the prophets,
- the Son of God,
- those that heard Christ, and
- the ministry of Paul, the Apostle to the Gentiles.

He comments on the Gospels and the Pauline epistles and has a lengthy section on the Acts of the Apostles, followed by one explaining why miraculous signs of the Acts period ceased.

A hard-back edition is available from **www.obt.org.uk** and from

The Open Bible Trust,
Fordland Mount, Upper Basildon,
Reading, RG8 8LU, UK.

A newly typeset book, well presented in an easy to read format, is available as a KDP paperback Amazon.

It is also available as an eBook from Amazon and Kindle

Further Reading

Joel's Prophecy: Past and Future
Michael Penny

Varying interpretations of Acts 2 have been the cause of many disagreements and rifts in Christendom. However, few have taken the time and trouble to study the prophecy from whom Peter quoted. Many know the five verses he quoted on the Day of Pentecost but ...

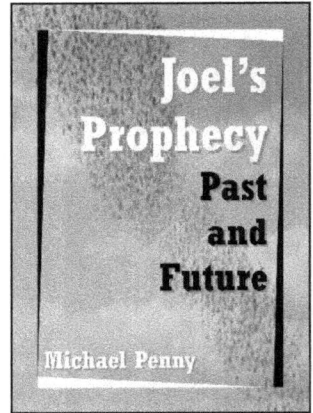

- What was the whole of Joel's message?
- What was the context of the words Peter quoted?
- What did Joel mean by them?
- What did Peter understand by them?
- Was Joel's prophecy fulfilled on the Day of Pentecost?
- Or are his words still unfulfilled?
- And if unfulfilled, when will they come to pass?

This book does an excellent job by first presenting the reader with an easy to read exposition of the whole of Joel's Prophecy. After that it moves on and discusses Peter's use of it, before considering whether or not Acts 2 was the fulfilment of what Joel wrote.

A paperback-back, perfect bound edition is available from
www.obt.org.uk and from

The Open Bible Trust,
Fordland Mount, Upper Basildon,
Reading, RG8 8LU, UK.

A newly typeset book, well presented in an easy to read format, is available as a KDP paperback Amazon.

It is also available as an eBook from Amazon and Kindle

About this book

The Bible

Interpretation ... Inspiration ... Right Division

The Bible is 'God breathed' and is 'profitable for doctrine, for reproof, for correction, for instruction in righteousness, that the man of God may be complete, thoroughly equipped for every good work' (2 Timothy 3:16-17).

However, although the Bible is 'for us' not all of the Bible is 'about us'. Thus we must first 'interpret' the Bible by seeking what it meant to the people to whom it was originally given.

Only after we have done that can we seek to 'apply' a passage to 21st century Christendom, and this is where the principle of 'right division' (2 Timothy 2:15) comes in.

Publications of The Open Bible Trust must be in accordance with its evangelical, fundamental and dispensational basis. However, beyond this minimum, writers are free to express whatever beliefs they may have as their own understanding, provided that the aim in so doing is to further the object of The Open Bible Trust. A copy of the doctrinal basis is available on **www.obt.org.uk** or from:

THE OPEN BIBLE TRUST
Fordland Mount, Upper Basildon,
Reading, RG8 8LU, UK.

www.ingramcontent.com/pod-product-compliance
Lightning Source LLC
Chambersburg PA
CBHW070555030426
42337CB00016B/2503